Echoes of a Country Heart

A COLLECTION OF STORY POEMS BY
BARBIE-JO SMITH
"A COUNTRY GAL IN THE CITY"

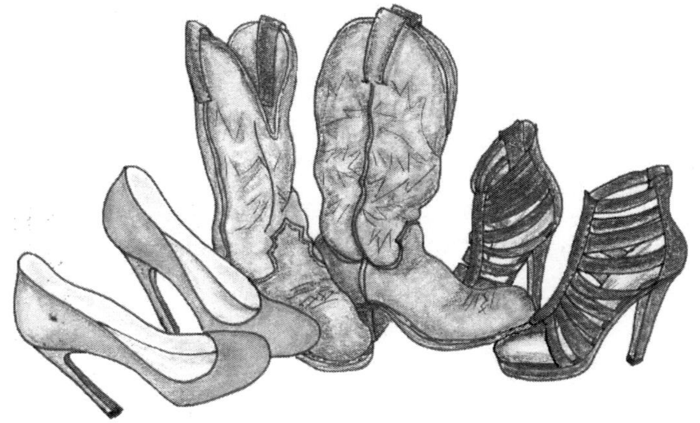

Dream Write Publishing Ltd.
P.O. Box 57083 RPO Eastgate
Sherwood Park AB T8A 5L7
www.dreamwritepublishing.ca

Echoes of a Country Heart
ISBN # 978-1-927510-69-8

Library and Archives Canada Cataloging in Publication
Echoes of a Country Heart
Smith, Barbie-Jo
Calgary AB

Printed in Edmonton AB Canada
www.images2go.com

Alpine Press LTD.

Foreword

I don't know why I love to write poetry—I just do. I find it challenging to tell a story with my words in rhyming format. More than that, however, I have discovered that I can often write about my deepest feelings more easily through poetry than through stories. My country roots go very deep. I hope my work will resonate with those of you have the extraordinary privilege of living on the land and that some of these poems will touch your heart and tickle your funny bone.

Barbie-Jo

Special thanks to my dear sister, Mary-Jane Smith Hale and her husband Frank Hale for allowing me to use pictures from their country home for the covers of this book.

I dedicate this book to my grandparents.
They were people of the land. Our roots grow very deep.

Hazel Davis Smith Lynch
James Arthur Smith
Kenneth Seymour Lynch

Mary Saunders Lawrence
Paul Robert Lawrence

My life is richer for all the times we spent together. I will always love you.

And .....

For Jamie who lives in my heart

For my dear husband, Dave, who understands what feeds my soul
and
lovingly supports me in all that I do.

"Love Never Fails"

Table of Contents

Echoes of a Country Heart

When the leaves turn golden in the autumn heat
And smoke hangs heavy in the air
The fields have ripened with amber wheat
My heat skips a beat and I whisper a prayer

I feel the call of my ancient roots
Telling me to do what my forbearers did
Gather the bounty of vegetables and fruits
To prepare for the winter months ahead

Cut and stook and winnow and glean
Salt and brine and pickle and dry
For old man winter is notoriously mean
And we need all our crops so we can get by

I want to knead and roll and crimp and bake
When the smell of autumn reaches my nose
Pies and breads and cookies and cake
And all the trimmings that with them go

When winter storms come and I'm safe in my chair
I'm ready, come blasting from your wintery home
I'm snug and warm and have a bounty to spare
So blow all you want for I'm safe, fed and warm

I think as I rock while the land soundly sleeps
And I plan for the harvest in the next year to come
When the crops that I've sown will be ready to reap
And I'll follow life's cycle all over again

... Barbie-Jo Smith

Pappy is the nickname I gave my husband, Dave. It just fits, especially when he's puttering with his tools or chopping wood. We love to have coffee in bed on cold winter mornings and take turns perking it and then bringing steaming cups of goodness to be enjoyed. With the blinds drawn up and the lights off, we watch the snow softly falling on the trees, while we snuggle under the covers and talk about the day to come.

I'll Put the Coffee On, Pappy

I'll put the coffee on, Pappy - It's been hours since we hit the hay
Sipping 'tween the sheets makes us happy - Till it's time to get on with the day

We'll talk about all sorts of subjects - Buried warm in our soft fuzzy covers
Our chats can be simple or complex - With many new things to discover

With fresh coffee warming our tummies - We may plan to camp or to fish
Or sit by the stream and play good old rummy - Just being together is our wish

Or maybe we'll plan what to grow - In the garden beside the greenhouse
How 'bout parsnips planted in a long row - By me and my darling old spouse

That's how it is with we elder ones - We chatter as much as we can
Ideas are born by the absolute tons - As we nestle together and plan

But soon it's time to get on with our chores - So we rise and start pulling on clothes
Sweatshirts and socks and don't forget drawers - What's in store for the day—who knows

That night we trade the events of the day - That made us so awfully darn happy
Now back in our warm bed we will soon lay - Till morn when the coffee's on Pappy

The bond between a working cowboy and his horse is a strong one born of respect, strength, courage comradeship, and, most of all, the love of the land.

My Cayuse Stands Waiting

Early dawn welcomes as I wake from my sleep
Warm sun rising tints the sky golden red
My boots leave a trail on the dew laden heath
As I button my shirt and head out to the shed

To the tack hut I wander to pick up my gear
My tawny old saddle well burnished by use
As I step out a whinny greets my ears
I turn and spot my faithful cayuse

Big brown eyes watch as I stroll towards his pen
His feet dance with joy; I reach for the gate
A low nicker of greeting between good friends
And over he trots; my old riding mate

Sun shines on his coat of rich velvet brown
I stroke his soft nose; "We're near ready," I say
A fist full of mane and a leap from the ground
I swing up on his back and we're off for the day

We'll spend hours together, my cayuse and I
Earning our keep out on the range
Checking on fences and riding cut lines
Counting new calves; shoot a coyote with mange

... Barbie-Jo Smith

After miles of work we take rest by the stream
I sip from my thermos; on the soft grass I lay
He drinks deeply from water so cool and so clean
And munches on wisps of early spring hay

From sunup to sunset we must be sharp like a knife
To do all sorts of work while we're out for the day
My cayuse and I are made for this life
Perfect work for us and seem just like play

Back home at the end of another long day
Twelve hours on the range; we're ready for rest
Cayuse looks forward to his flakes of sweet hay
While I cook my supper then slick up my mess

This is our life, old cayuse and me
We're both tough as leather but softies inside
Two of a kind, wild and free
With mutual affection, loyalty and pride

Warm by my hearth after our day
I glance out the window and what do I see
Equally weary at the end of his day
But ....
My cayuse stands waiting for tomorrow with me

There were three children in our family and Jamie was the best of us all.

The Last Time I Saw Him

He wore his buckskin jacket with long fringes of soft brown
His blonde hair sparkled in the sun; on his collar it fell down
His leather cowboy boots scuffed the dusty country track
But something in me sensed that he was never coming back

He was tall and lean in his well-worn and faded jeans
His broad shoulders shaped his shirt; he still looked just like a teen
He sauntered to his truck parked on the dusty, gravelly ground
He raised his hand in silent wave and then he turned around

What was in that one last wave that made my heart grow cold
He was young and strong and handsome, and very smart and bold
But in that silent instant as he drove on down the road
I knew his life would be cut short, his story left untold

He was the very best of men, loyal and always true
There didn't seem to be anything that he couldn't easily do
A family man with loving wife and baby sons so wee
He had everything to live for, his family and for me

And so it was that fate stepped in and took him from this world
Far too soon I told myself, my heart a painful swirl
Of losing him and missing the fine man that he was
His death was cloaked in mystery; there was no certain cause

... Barbie-Jo Smith

He was my dearest brother and I miss him every day
Even after all these years since he went away
I can hear his laugh and see his smile across these many years
Sometimes it catches me unaware and brings on waves of tears

But I know in my heart that he really is ok
And he travels with me through each and every day
He's also in a safe place where he looks down on us all
This quiet man, my brother James, forever young and tall

The last time I saw him he was striding young and strong
Looking like our next visit wouldn't be so very long
And in truth I guess it won't 'cause time goes by so fast
And one day soon we'll laugh and chat, together then at last

James Arthur Smith
1957 - 1987

This poem was inspired by the ongoing war that we had with the squirrels in the yard and the damage they did. One day we captured a young nursing mother. We had a complete attitude change when we realized that she had just as much right to live as we did.

She was just being herself—a squirrel. It was a lesson well learned.

Varmint Trap

He rubbed his palms together, eyes bright with silent joy,
As he looked out towards the trap set back along the fence.
Wondering what wee varmint was drawn to his decoy,
He could hardly stand the waiting to ease his great suspense.

Walking across the turf he knew he had to harden,
So he thought back over years about the damage,
To the beloved plants he tended in his lovely backyard garden,
When just one squirrel could run a terrible rampage.

As he neared the cage staccato chattering began,
And the squirrel scolded loudly for this deed.
Racing around the cage and then on hind legs he would stand,
Then the man saw something he should heed.

Standing up on hind legs and begging to get out,
Revealed the underbelly of this tiny little squirrel.
The man could see evidence of which there was no doubt,
That this little guy was really a wee girl.

... Barbie-Jo Smith

It was obvious that she had some babies snugly tucked away.
He guessed a nest in some nearby tall tree.
She must have dashed out quickly to eat something fresh that day,
And now all she needed was to be set free.

The man stood watching her and pondered all the maybes.
This isn't really fair he told himself.
But the right thing was to let her go and return her to her babies.
This furry tiny chattering elf.

And that's exactly what happened and then he did another thing.
Took the trap down then and packed it all away.
This little one deserves to live and through the trees to swing,
And chatter and gather and run and play.

So now the man sits on his porch with peanuts in his hand,
Till all his tiny furry friends appear.
The babies are growing fast and they're really very grand.
His right decision has filled his life with cheer.

How many of us have gone through what this old cowboy has? No matter what walk of life one comes from, as we get older, we seem to struggle with ever-changing technology. I think that's why God made grandchildren. They're just a phone call away and they "get it"!

Cowboy HD

My knees are hurtin' and my face is red,
From a-bending in two and standin' on my head.
I'm a-stringin' a wire for the new TV,
So we can watch "The Duke" from our bed, you see.

The good woman said, "Get that thaaaang a hooked up."
So I grabbed the tool box from my old pickup truck,
And I entered the battle with technology,
So we can enjoy our big new-fangled TV.

I'm a-tempted to call up our oldest grandchild,
Who is a savvy techno kid, a-puttin' it mild.
But pride is a-keepin' me from a makin' that call.
Though we all know that pride goes before the big fall!

And fall I will if I don't get this done.
Oh, technology is tough for this old western son,
But the need to see "The Duke" on HDTV,
Is a-stronger than the urge to keep my sanity.

Still grinding away, I'm a-struggling with them cords.
Holy cow, this is tough! But I sense a great reward.
I'm a-conquerin' this problem as I take another look.
I guess it works better usin' the instruction book.

And suddenly the problem is a problem no more.
We're a-hooked up and ready and I never even swore.
Here comes the popcorn in a huge round bowl,
Just in time for the movie. Phew; reached my goal!

So here we are a-loungin' and a-waitin' for the show,
Chattin' all 'bout the westerns we both love and know.
Whoever thought we'd have an HDTV?
Now here comes "The Duke". Yee-haw, glory be!

I've often wondered what bulls think when a rider climbs up on their backs.

Get off My Back!

A long time ago when I was a calf
Out on the wide open range
My friends and I would gambol and laugh
Never dreaming that soon we would change

We'd galloped down to the bull pen
And listen to their exciting stories
About how they bucked off the riding men
When they were in their glory

It seemed a fancy life they had led
And I wanted it with all my young bovine heart
They said, "work your muscles and stay well fed
And you'll get your chance for a start"

I grew up strong with thick horns like stone
Much taller than all the rest
My muscles were hard with balance and tone
And I put all of my friends to the test

One day a man came and took me away
To a place where brave bulls got to buck
A rodeo, I overheard him say
For me a stroke of good luck

I had heard of these places where bulls buck off men
Who tried to stay on at great length
The older bulls told us when down in the pens
Now I was the one would show off my strength

... Barbie-Jo Smith

There were the cowboys who would ride on my back
An outlandish thing for a brave brute
The first dude jumped on and gave me a whack
And I blasted right out of the chute

Did he think that I was a simple old horse?
Sitting up high on my back
It felt pretty silly to me, of course
Then he gave me another loud thwack

My anger rose high to a fever pitch
As my pride was bruised to the core
I shifted and bucked to get him to shift
Oh, tomorrow, this dude would be sore

But he stuck in his seat like he was part of me
And I started to worry and fret
I had to regain my bull's pride don't you see
So I bucked even harder yet

Pitching and swerving I gave a great snort
The dude shook a bit by this blast
Then with one giant heave, my final resort
He slipped off balance at last

Oh now I had him, a boost to my pride
As he swayed to my final huge thrust
But the damage was done, he had started to slide
And quite soon he'd be eating my dust

He was well on his way to losing his seat
I felt the rope round my body go slack
The cowboy flew over my head as I leaped
And my bull lips yelled

Get off my back!

In loving memory of all the wonderful fathers who have gone to heaven.

A Hero is at Peace

Memories move gently across all of our minds
As they brush the shadows of space and time
Years flown by and now they have ceased
For a wonderful man who is now at peace

He was just like us in the way that he lived
Did his very best to work and to willingly give
To his God, his family, and communities he loved
And now he's gone home on the wings of a dove

Good qualities were many: he was always prepared
To use knowledge and talent and willingly share
With anyone, always gave a fair shake
Saying, "To you, from my heart, whatever it takes."

He wore many hats throughout his career
Walked in high places for many good years
But he also loved nature: the simplicity she gave
His heart ever stalwart, true and brave

... Barbie-Jo Smith

He was a proud Canadian who lived by his creed
Do your best in all things: show no avarice or greed
Stand tall and be proud wherever you be
Protecting our country and keeping it free

He was a hero to all in his long time on earth
A mentor, a teacher, a man of great worth
We are poorer by far now that he's passed
For there are few like him left: men of great class

We're grateful for all the time that we had
To have known this great man who was my wonderful Dad
His memory forever engraved in our minds
This fine man who was simply one of a kind

I love you Dad.
I miss you every day.
I hold you close to my heart.

Who remembers the outhouse? Ours was a "two-holer". My brother was a little boy when the new outhouse was built. My mother was afraid he'd fall in so she drilled a small hole between the big ones into which she put a big red funnel—the type used to change oil in a car—it worked like a charm!

Behind the Lilac Hedge

She lives behind the lilac hedge in the corner of the yard
Her clean slim lines are elegant; she stands tall and proud
She's waiting for her visitors who come throughout the day
They know that she's essential but they really never stay

She's as modern as they come with new boards of stained chartreuse
Two stations are within for her welcome guests to use
Several catalogues are there with pages set to tear
To help conclude their business or to read, which is quite rare

She knows she serves a purpose but still her heart is low
She yearns for them to spend their time there, lazy, long and slow
But when they come to visit, it's always too brief a time
Even though she's hidden by the hedge and flowering vines

She's always been there to serve them in good times and in bad
When Johnny had the stomach flu for him she was quite sad
And when Grandma's pie didn't agree there was a rowdy hearty group
Who trotted to her private comfort and relief so they could p.......

... Barbie-Jo Smith

She's seen and heard a lot of things, and she never tells a soul
When Annie sat crying within when she felt like such a fool
Or when James was so excited about his much deserved win
She wished she had a face so he could see her proud grin

There were times when she bore the brunt of many cruel jokes
About her purpose and her value to all the local folks
Even the thought of being yanked away, thrown upon her back
Onto a passing train to take her far away, way down its steely track

Or uprooting her by a few feet, exposing her great pit
So someone innocent would fall right in, which seemed to be great wit
By those who didn't realize her value and her use
Employ her to hurt others; there was just no good excuse

Mostly though she's happy to be a welcome, silent host
Just by being there when they all need her the most
Despite jokes about her and the threat of technology
She proud to serve her family just who she wants to be

Our Precious Outhouse.

The inspiration for this poem was memories of trying to get a pump started when it has lost its prime and you urgently needed to get the water flowing. Then there's the relief when it finally gives a cough and chugs to life. Only then can you wander up to the house for a well-earned coffee break!

Priming the Pump

Turn the pump on, darling
'Cause we need to water the cows
They're down in the pasture a-bawling
They want a cool drink right now

That ornery old pump needs priming
And a darn good kick with a boot
But with some cranking and tricky timing
It will leap into action and work

The bulls are watching the ladies
Down in the lush grassy pasture
While the ladies are feeding their babies
It's all part of the beauty of nature

But if you want to eat beef in cold weather
We'd better get cracking this morning
I'll get the hoses, saddle up and slap leather
You bring the tools 'cause that pump is a calling

We've coaxed it along these many long years
'Cause it's really just like an old friend
As it pumps out sweet water for heifers and steers
Why it works, we don't comprehend

With a lot of hard work and portion of cussing
The pump jumps to life with a sputtering cough
The cows hear the roar and start lowing and fussing
And head trotting towards the field trough

Now we've got that pump working, Pappy
So things are as good as can be
The cattle are watered and happy
Pie and coffee for you and for me

In an archive picture, with number 307 pinned on her fancy shirt, a young Aboriginal girl waited to compete at a rodeo. Her exquisite face made me want to know who she was and where she is now.

Buffalo Girl: Queen of the Rodeo

All gussied up for Stampede Week
With fancy tooled boots and denim jeans
Buckskin and spurs; cowgirl chic
Ready for the chance to fulfill her dreams

She's the daughter of the earth
From a culture old and true
A person of great worth
In her fancy shirt of blue

Her people once roamed all over the land
In long ages before this huge show
Her world now straddles two cultures grand
And she'll show us all she knows

Her high stepping dance in a jingle dress
Hand-made design with shawl, bone and beads
But today she'll compete in a gruelling test
Barrel racing on her strong, steady steed

... Barbie-Jo Smith

Her face represents proud people of old
Buffalo Girl, the name in her heart
Stoic and strong and brave and bold
Number 307; ready to start

So it's wild excitement for this young girl's ride
As she spurs her mount into the show
She'll demonstrate all her skill with pride
This Queen of the Rodeo

Where is she now; this girl from the past
Did she win a prize on her prairie cayuse
Or is it only her picture that lasts
And she's but a memory for us to hold close

Or maybe the years have gone by in a blur
Her memories held deeply within her
The girl from both worlds with the courage of two
In her crisp fancy shirt of turquoise blue

The mystery girl we were not meant to know
But she's still... The Queen of the Rodeo

This poem speaks for itself, about the eternal love that a mother has for her children.

Linda's Mom

When my friend Linda's mother passed
An angel rose gently towards the sky
She was freed of her pain at long last
Then slipped homewards like the breath of a sigh

She left her family on this earthly plane
And went to do her heavenly chores
Nevermore feeling the crushing pain
Of her body's strength sapped to her core

And leaving behind her family dear
On this earth to wonder how
They will live without her always near
But she silently made to them a vow

I'll be with you always, my precious dears
No matter what life brings or takes away
Live your lives without any fears
For close to you I will always stay

Look for me when the sun shines bright
Or when the stars come out and shine at night

… Barbie-Jo Smith

When the stallion thunders across the grass
Or when the geese, in fall, flutter softly past

When the tulips bloom in early spring
And the robins come back and just for you sing

When the snowflakes tumble to the ground
New courage for you will soon be found

When the loon calls only to your heart
That is when your deepest healing will start

Watch for my signs as you walk down life's road
I'll be beside you to lighten your load
My love will support you in all that you try
Dry your tears now; Be happy; Don't cry

She gazed down from heaven as they talked about her
You'll be fine she whispered; I love you, my dears
She dabbed a small tear, smiled, and then she went on
But her love lives inside them ….. On and on and on

Who among us doesn't love a sunflower standing bright yellow gloriously tall over the garden? They seem to be the gathering place and a source of food for so many, giving pleasure for a long summer.

Sunflower

Her lovely green and yellow dress
Shines cool and crisp and clear
Wearing fashion's latest trends
Draws bees to hover near

Birds flock to her gorgeous face
While tall and straight she stands
She's elegant and full of grace
As she looks out on her land

She needs the bees to visit her
To linger and pollinate
They're drawn in a frantic buzzing blur
Her yellow face is their bait

All summer she's busy making her seeds
So by fall she can spread her crop
Food for many creatures' needs
As they grow then ripen and drop

At the end to summer's long hot days
She casts her seeds; a signal that brings
Bittersweet feelings that come my way
But ......
She'll be back again next spring

... Barbie-Jo Smith

This poem was inspired by my wonderful father's last hours. While my heart still aches for his loss, I was extraordinarily blessed to have had that time with him. He was one of a kind and I look forward to seeing him again one day soon.

The Room Was Dark and Quiet

The room was dark and quiet
On her lashes grew a tear
His breathing came in shallow sighs
So she knew the end was near

She thought about the day before
They had chatted for so long
About times they had and so much more
Now they both needed to be strong

She gazed down at his well, worn hands
That had served him throughout his days
Had built things with his clever plans
And taught her his giving ways

Her mind roamed back through all the years
Sweet family times of old
Laughter, sunshine and, yes, some tears
She felt his hands growing cold

His blue eyes could no more summon the sight
Of the beauty of his special day
For now his heart slid towards the light
And it was time to drift away

His breathing grew quite shallow
As he gave her one last grin
She swore she saw a beauteous light
Glow over his faded skin

Then before her eyes she felt him leave
And was thankful for all that she had
She knew she would take a long time to grieve
This fine man she called her Dad

Most of us have had a pet that touched our hearts deeply. This poem reminds us that it really doesn't matter what one looks like, but how you live your life and that you know the value of true friendship.

Buddy

He's not much to look at but he's hardy and tough
The blood of many breeds runs through his veins
He's tall at the shoulder with a collie-like ruff
And the way that he is just fits his name

One eye is bright blue and one is deep brown
A red golden tail is the flag that he flies
A topknot of head curls looks like a crown
And his big feet work well despite their great size

... Barbie-Jo Smith

He's part pointer, part herder, and part hound all in one
This handsome pal who walks by my side
In the blink of an eye he'll break into a run
To chase down a varmint, tongue lolling, mouth wide

One summer he saved me from a smelly collision
As a skunk took a shortcut next to my chair
Buddy barked a sharp warning and I made a decision
To sit still till our guest ambled back to his lair

As summer was ending one hot August day
A small neighbour boy took a fall in my lake
Buddy jumped in and saved him, paddling away
Scooping him out like a big canine rake

He's a wonder on four legs on all types of trails
He can herd, he can hunt and can run without end
His talents are many; he just never fails
But most wondrous to me; he's my very best friend

We're a good match together, old Buddy and me
We've worked through the years side by side
He knows me so well I have to agree
I look over to him with a heart full of pride

Now we're both grey haired and at times don't remember
Our chores as before around the old farm
Most times we sit quietly by the fire and just slumber
Content with our memories, safe, snug and warm

But.... Then there is that once in a lifetime pet that walks right into your heart and her loss is almost too much to bear, except for the knowledge that you will be together again in heaven.

You Can Chase Gophers Forever Now

Today my best friend had to go and with her went my heart
Her body just wore out and pain was always there
My heart broke when I knew it was time we had to part
And to let her go in peace was to show how much I care

She looked into my eyes with the trust she always had
And I stood tall to do the hard thing and take away her pain
My heart hurts at her loss and I'm profoundly sad
Because I'll never have my forever friend by my side again

The hours we spent together in the field beside the town
Where she sniffed and rolled and ran to her doggie heart's delight
Gophers sounded alarm when they knew she was around
Then she'd stand and sniff the wind—what a glorious sight

Her fur was golden red and her tail was like a plume
Her eyes were deep brown like the soft skin of a doe
Thick blonde ruff rippling as she'd dance around the room
Lolling tongue in doggie laugh—she loved her family so

... Barbie-Jo Smith

She loved to lean into my legs, feeling my gentle pat
Rumbling deep within her chest at the pleasure that she felt
Then sliding down my legs and turning on her back
Telling me to scratch her belly while my heart would simply melt

Her temperament was soft and she had a kindly way
She was never, ever rough when she was with the kids
But once, for me she put herself directly in harm's way
When a vicious dog came charging out; she put him on the skids

She came into our lives as a golden ball of fur
And fit right in our family right from the wonderful start
The years went by as they do in an awful speeding blur
Yielding her to age and pain, till we finally had to part

She simply loved her family and we all loved her right back
It's so hard to be without her; she was such a part of me
But she had to go and be with her special heavenly pack
Where there's no more pain, she's ok and she's running fast and free

I love you Mae. I miss you. Rest easy, girl.
You can chase gophers forever now.

A dear friend of mine lost her husband two years ago. They had everything to live for and he was far too young to die. She has worked very hard to deal with his loss and recently had the courage to sell their home and start a new life. Those of us who have lived through this experience will recognize this bittersweet journey.

New Home

The pictures are down from the soft colored walls
And I survey my home; rooms, floors and halls
The kitchen is empty of all pots and pans
And most things are already packed in the van

I saunter through rooms where we lived for these years
To check for forgotten bits of my heart
Good-bye to my memories with a few salty tears
For here they must stay; I've a new life to start

Most of the objects that I hold very dear
Have already gone to my new little nest
Where I'll hang them and place them and polish them clear
Till my new home is looking its best

I look over my shoulder and glance back once more
Will I miss this old place; my heart bittersweet
Then leaving forever and closing the door
I walk towards my new life with fresh memories to greet

... Barbie-Jo Smith

My husband, Dave, makes great jelly we enjoy on toast with cowboy coffee in the morning. He also makes three alarm salsa and feather light cheese biscuits. Dave's talents have allowed me to abdicate my role as queen of the kitchen.

Pappy's Making Jelly

Pappy's in the kitchen with the big pot a' boiling
Making juicy berry jelly for our toast
I'm sitting back as I watching him a' toiling
And that's the part that I like the most

Brewing and stirring and tasting and a' grinnin'
He's creating a sweet and tasty treat
He had it all figured out right from the beginnin'
And it's going to taste terrific and so sweet

As the jam cooks down his concentration grows intensely
As he stirs and hums and tests
My eagerness to taste rises in me immensely
I think this batch is going to be his best

Ready and cooled and ladled from the pot
Rosy red jelly for our breakfast toast
With a cup of cowboy coffee sipped while it's hot
What better breakfast can one boast.

I'm a proud country gal who loves her man you see
He can hunt, fish, shoot, dig and rake
But when he's in the kitchen he's got talent more than me
'Cause his berry jelly really takes the cake.

This trilogy is a tribute to the beautiful Canadian Prairies. Together they are known as the Prairie Provinces, but separately they are as diverse as each one of us. If you have the chance, travel throughout these provinces, meeting the people, seeing the landscape and being thankful, as I am, that they stand as the strong triad of economic growth, power, diversity, and breathtaking beauty.

The Land That I Call Home

Manitoba
Cree name meaning
"Straits of Manitou, the great spirit"

Born as a pivotal place in our land
Where the courier des bois and voyageurs were kings
Opening trade routes to connect to the great west
They joined the provinces with their courage and strength

Two inland seas and a port on Hudson Bay
Make Manitoba a leader in fishing and trade
Boreal forests, Canadian shield, mighty rivers
That served as the highways for les courageous voyageurs

Proud native peoples blended with newcomers
To make a great nation called Métis
Scots and French traders joined in their toils
To promote the Hudson Bay Company

Fields of grain stand tall in their glory
Sun sends its golden rays to ripen the bounty
One of three provinces that feed the world's people
Bread basket of our land, proud and strong

... Barbie-Jo Smith

Far northern reaches where ancient ones still live
Ocean home of beluga and the great polar bear
Rich in the fur trade, next door to the wild north
Where caribou still run in herds of thousands

Great southern prairies where Red River carts
Brought people who sought the promise of freedom
To make a new life and bring their old ways
Adding to our country's rich cultural diversity

Manitoba: gateway to the west
Forests, fisheries, icebergs, and grain crops

Part of my life
Part of my soul

Saskatchewan
Cree word meaning
"Swift flowing river"

Huge province, long and wide
Place of great fishing and plentiful wild game
The most underestimated province in Canada
Full of coulees, lakes, dinosaur tracks, and breathtaking beauty

Wide sweeping grain fields
Rolling hills and coulees
Rich boreal forest teeming with animals
Wild rushing rivers run straight to the sea

Many resources make this province rich
Potash, oil, logging, tourism, farming, fur trade
Home to diversity of cultures and talents
Ribbons of highway join rich urban splendour to small friendly towns

Put your ear to the ground and hear the old ones
Dancing to bring on the buffalo hunt
Kneel and pray with the Mennonite families
Who farm in all regions to this day

Rushing water tumbles over great dams
Corralling water into huge lakes
Where people can work and play altogether
While the sun caresses the crops while they grow

Wild wolf and tall elk call in the evening
To hearts long connected to Mother Earth
Great herds of grazing cattle offer their harvest
While huge hog operations fill tables across the land

Look to the sky and see thousands of geese
Ride on a roundup or canoe down the rivers
Walk through the wheat field on a hot summer day
Fish in the rivers and hunt in the autumn

Land of the Living Skies
Part of my soul

Alberta
Named for Princess Louise Alberta

A place where wild bison still roam
Through coulees and forested stands of the north
Walking where their ancestors ran
To the beat of their hooves over ancient land

... Barbie-Jo Smith

Black gold is king in this bustling province
Giving jobs, feeding families all over the land
A gift from those creatures that lived long ago
Crawled, ran, flew, and swam

Dinosaurs walked on this land in the past
Leaving their prints that they once ruled the world
Walk in the canyons on any fine day
And discover the past laying right at your feet

Proud native peoples: the backbone of this wild land
Came up from the old ways into modern times
Tribes of strength, knowledge, and courage
Now thrive side by side with ones from new land

Vast fields of golden wheat sway in the wind
In contrast with yellow fields of canola
Crops share the land with oil derricks
That give economic promise to the people

Foothills gently roll to the west
Giving way to Rocky Mountains that bring
The snow eater—chinook—to change the air
Leaving spring where winter once stood

Great herds of cattle graze in the sun
And feed the world with premium protein
Land of many people who work together
To make the best of everything

Province of my birth
Part of my soul

There are things to which we are all born and we are destined to be. No matter how it may seem to us, we all have a place in this world.

Lobo

Along the ridge and howling his cry
Flat out against the cool breeze
He follows the scent of game close by
That he will catch and dispatch with ease

His ebony coat blends with the dark of the night
As he stretches with widening strides
His prey, a young doe, in frenzied wild flight
Fleeing quickly to stay alive

He can run on it seems for hour after hour
On his quest to capture a meal
She can match him for speed but not his sheer power
She senses him close to her heels

His lips are drawn back showing jagged white teeth
Designed to disable and tear
Her long legs propel her through the low sandy heath
Her soft liquid eyes full of fear

The laws of the earth roar in both of their minds
To live, eat, and breed—their kinds to fulfil
She comes from the forest of lush grass and pines
While he was born to kill

The scent of her flesh keeps him close to her track
She pauses to maybe hear his soft prowl
He leaps from the ridge down onto her back
He tears at her flesh with a savage growl

Her eyes are glazed over with shock and surprise
As he sinks fangs deep into her throat
He howls with delight at his hard earned prize
As her blood trickles down her soft coat

He surveys the glen with his bold amber eyes
The law of the forest in him deeply revives
One has to die and one stays alive
For only the strongest survive

Lobo

I wore my petite open-toe sparkly shoes to a dance one night. The music was country-fabulous and I danced up a storm until a size 12 cowboy boot stomped right on the top of my foot! Not long after that, I took myself to the doctor who treated me for almost a year until I was in dancing form again! This poem is for him.

My Feet Don't Hurt Anymore

My feet don't hurt anymore
No more do I limp and groan
When I'm heading out the door
Or running for the phone

Do you know what this means to me
Freedom from constant pain
I'm allowed to run and just be
Never to worry again

If I do my part to take good care
Of my feet from heel to toe
Then they will take me anywhere
In the world I want to go

I'm not sad to say good-bye
To constant pain and woe
Now when my tootsies hit the floor
I'm ready and raring to go

I never realized how much pain I knew
Until it was gone evermore
Hallelujah! Put on my dancing shoes
'Cause my feet don't hurt anymore

Neighbours are important, especially to those who live in the country. When the chips are down, neighbours depend each other, and when the hard work is done, neighbours are there to celebrate.

My Aching Head

Last night I went visiting my neighbours towards the west
Sporting my good cowboy boots and fancy leather vest
My horse was all combed out and prancing very high
We cut a pretty spiffy look, old Buster and I

The journey was a long one so we planned to stay all night
Buster in the barn chomping hay to his delight
I was put up for the night by my neighbour friends
What on earth happened between beginning and the end

The plan was a good one till the fat got in the fire
Who knows how it happened but it surely was a mire
Good home cooking and nips of brew couldn't cause much trouble
But things went downhill promptly and I was quickly seeing double

My neighbour is a good man with an awfully pretty wife
They are the salt of the earth and a pleasure in my life
Always giving to their friends, they never would deprive
What on earth happened so soon after I arrived

I wish I could remember where it all went rather wrong
Perhaps the case of brew we downed while singing cowboy songs
Whatever caused this blank in time, my memory has gone AWOL
However, my instinct tells me that we surely had a ball

This morning I have a headache and its hurting, oh so, bad
It's a big one and it throbs just like the worst I've ever had
Pounding like a hammer inside my weary head
Makes me yearn to be at home in my soft and cozy bed

What would cause a pain like this so achingly complete
It hurts all over from my head down to my size 12 feet
Could it be the six-pack that I guzzled late last night
Oh no, I don't think so, cuz the taste was just so right.

Perhaps, it was the pizza with all the extra cheese
So spicy and delicious that I asked for extras please
Oh no, it couldn't be, cuz it was a homemade treat
Hot and fresh with big thick crust and lots and lots of meat

I wonder if it might have been the garlic sausage ring
Fried in golden butter and served with sour cream
No! Those foods are wholesome and full of nutrients
It's a mystery to my stomach from where this pain was sent

Then there was the homemade wine to toast a meal this grand
Followed by the liqueur, which was an obscure brand
I had to have my manners so I drank and ate all night
Could this be what caused my sensitivity to light

To end the night my host fried perogies served on bread.
I stuffed them down and knew it was time to go to bed
But I was just so tired that I flaked out on the floor
Snuggled tight with blankets I soon began to snore

That brings us to this morning and I'm feeling awfully ill
While I'm standing straight and tall, I'm hurting badly still
It's time to head on out and down the lane, of course
I would do that promptly if I could only find my horse

I left him in the barn with the other stock last night
He couldn't have wandered off as the door was closed up tight
Where on earth could Buster be; I need to get on home
I'm worried quite a bit by now as he really likes to roam

But what's that shuffle that I hear at the back of this old barn
Creeping closer I can see a hulking sorrel form
It's Buster and it looks to me that he really needs the pill
'Cause he's been lapping up the runoff from my neighbours whiskey still

Despite our illness, it's long past time that we were heading home
Me hanging on the neck of my faithful, drunken roan
The equine stumbling down the lane and me a human mess
Do you think last evening was the cause of our distress

Buster staggered across the field and soon we were at home
Where we'll stay for quite some time, not wanting more to roam
Buster, well he hit the hay, soon asleep right on his feet
And I snored loudly in my soft bed snuggled in my sheets

Tomorrow, I'll be sipping coffee before dawn
Buster will amble from the barn doing a horsey yawn
Will I learn a lesson not to end up in a mess
I suppose until the next time my neighbour calls, I guess

Never judge a book by its cover. Guardian angels come in all forms.

The Tattoo and the Cross

He strode into my country store like he was on a quest
A giant of a man dressed in a tooled black leather vest
His neck was tattooed with words I did not understand
As if his feelings were stamped there as a kind of open brand

On his head he wore a doo-wrap and under that a braid
That hung between his shoulders like a golden warning flag
Something in him scared me but I also sensed his pain
That this tough man carried something I could not explain

His beard was full and red, hanging way down on his shirt
His boots were scuffed and worn, and covered with road dirt
But his jeans were clean and pressed and I wondered at the contrast
With the tattoos on his arms like an angry knife slash

He glanced at me and nodded and then he strode away
To the back where the coolers were and there he seemed to stay
While I watched him keenly not really knowing why
Another man stepped through the door; said "Hold your hands up high"

This new man was clean cut but in his hands he held a gun
My heart leaped into my mouth; I thought to turn and run
He was very calm and seemed to know what he was doing
Despite his good looks I felt the evil that was cruelly brewing

His cool blue eyes fixed me and then his voice rasped out to me
Give me all your money and then you will be free
My shaking hands went to the till to scoop up all the cash
But before I could do what he said there came a mighty crash

His gun went flying from his hands as he sprawled upon the floor
The tattooed stranger stood over him ready to do more
The thief gazed up and a strange look came across his face
He sensed his life was changed and was standing amid grace

I looked at the tattooed man then back towards the crook
Energy ran between them as the downed man's body shook
While his face began to shine in light I've not seen before
Tears ran down his face as he lay there on the floor

A white light filled the room while a mighty central shaft
Shone down on the tattooed man as he chuckled and then laughed
He pulled the crook to his feet; put an arm around his back
Said, "You've fallen into sin, my son, but now you're back on track"

They both turned to look my way and I gave a little start
I saw the light of God in them and felt it in my heart
The thief said he was sorry and asked if I'd forgive
I knew I would remember this day as long as I would live

The answer was yes, of course; he had really done no harm
As he turned to leave the store I glanced down upon his arm
A tattoo suddenly appeared as if it was embossed
A simple design in plain black; it was a holy cross

I turned to the bearded man with a question on my lips
He smiled at me with huge green eyes; his hands upon his hips
"My dear one, what you first see isn't always what you think"
Have faith that God's angels are around you serving as his link

"I was sent to help you in your hour of need
We come in all sizes, races, colours and, yes, creeds
Don't be fooled by looks or thoughts on how a man should seem
It's what's inside his heart that counts and how he lives life's dream"

I looked more closely and saw his tattoos right up close
The beauty was so stunning that my jumbled thoughts just froze
A cross emblazoned on his neck was not an ugly slash
There was no doubt he was an angel; I knew it in a flash

He turned to leave but before he walked away
He said my life was ever changed by what happened on this day
This tattooed man from God's right hand softly touched my face
And said, "God dwells in all of us. You always have his grace"

When you stand quietly, sometimes the most exquisite things happen.

Stallion

He glides across the back woods ridge over crumbling mountain scree
Then I watch his body disappear behind the huge pine trees
Did I really see him there before he wheeled around to flee
Or was it my imagination yearning just to see

Again I glimpse his tawny body flashing through the trees
And then he bursts from behind some rocks and stops to gaze at me
Our eyes meet and time stands still; hearts pound excitedly
Then he tosses his head and paws the ground kicking up the soft debris

His long tail flies out in the wind as he moves down from the trees
His hoofs are swift as he gallops towards me like a golden wild banshee
Then suddenly he's there in front so near that I can see
The copper glints within his eyes that are looking straight at me

He steps towards me with caution, this creature wild and free
His head goes down to sniff my cheek and his soft nose tickles me
As I slowly move my arm up and with my hand touch carefully
He rumbles deep from within his chest as if he's very pleased

I stroke his nose and then his neck and he stands very still for me
As if he knows I am filled with awe but also quite small and wee
This wonder of nature towers there, a gift for me to see
And we both enjoy our visit as the sun rises over the trees

I whisper little words of love to this creature I'm thrilled to see
I am no longer afraid of him for he's gentle and will not flee
He's content to feel my touch and stand quietly beside me
Just the two of us for a while, filled with wondrous glee

And then with one great snort he turns and makes a sign to leave
I understand that he must return to collect his mares and breed
For he is the one who guides them and it's to his strong decree
That the life of the herd will be in his foals that he sires prodigiously

I am awed by the wonder and the rare chance that suddenly has been
To see this wild creature that spent some quiet time with me
And as I watch him gallop to his herd I simply must agree
That my heart will ever be with him dancing wild and free

Autumn is my favourite time of year. Harvest is a time of taking in and preparing for the long winter ahead. It's a time of thankfulness for the bounty of the land and the ability to reap it. It's a time to understand the cycles of all our lives.

Harvest

The smell of fall is earthy and grand
As my feet tread across the black soil
The first day of harvest is here at hand
And the tractor needs greasing and oil

My boys rose early for today they begin
To combine the fields that lay ripe and ready
They sit tall at the cab; the hot sun on their skin
While their strong arms keep tractor wheels steady

... Barbie-Jo Smith

Three generations go out into the fields
Granddad remembers dust covered their faces
Working together to bring good yields
While hard working Clydesdales toiled in their traces

Man and beast worked hard each day
To bring in the crop for wintertime's food
Sun beating down on their backs while they hayed
Or running for cover when the hail rolled on through

Now they work just as hard with more land to swath
Keep huge equipment churning the grain
I take them their meals in the back of the truck
A few minutes of rest before going again

At the end of the harvest is time for a rest
When we're thankful for all our good fortune
We rest and visit and dressed in our best
We dance and enjoy 'neath a harvest moon

So this is our life and we'll have nothing else. We're rooted securely right here on our land.
Proud generations have worked it before us.
No offer of riches would be enough to make us leave this place we call home
Where our people are buried.
As long as we can, we'll be out early in the spring to sow the seed
Then back in the fall to gather our crops,
For the cycle of the crops is also the cycle of our lives.

This poem is inspired by that feeling of awakening that comes when the harsh winter weather gives away to a gentler breeze bringing the promise of renewed life.

Spring Comes Again

Spring is a friend who slowly arrives
Over land that for too long was covered with snow
Her warm sun encourages trees to revive
And start their new cycle when sap starts to flow

Little plants, too, feel her warm gentle touch
As they peek out of cool thawing ground
Small pansy faces give my heartstrings a clutch
And my memories of spring soon abound

The urge to dig soil and plant new things there
Is strong and I want to give in to my whims
But for now I must stay in my cozy deck chair
For it's not quite the time to begin

Spring will arrive in her own special way
As she has done in the past for long ages
Cool early winds keep her warm sun at bay
So her magic unfolds in slow stages

But I am impatient for warm ground to sow
All the seeds for a summer array
But when Spring is ready I'm sure that I'll know
Till then in my chair I will stay

... Barbie-Jo Smith

There are nights when my mind is full of creative ideas. Sleep is elusive and the best thing I can do is get up and sit quietly in thought until I have listened to my creative heart and sleep returns.

Some Nights I Walk the Floors

Moonlight falls softly across the floor by the bed where I'm trying to sleep
But I lay awake with my thoughts this night; there's no use in counting sheep
My mind is alive with thoughts that I struggle to sort through in some form
It seems no use to stay laying there even though I'm snug and warm

I peel back the quilt and slide out from my safe and warm cocoon
Then slip on my housecoat and slowly creep out of our room
I am careful to be quiet so you can sleep on in your dream filled world
I touch your cheek softly as your stir; pull covers round as you lay curled

I walk one by one through darkened rooms touching familiar things
Objects, possessions, impressions; they all have a story to bring
Some call warm tears to my eyes and some call up a wee smile
As I walk the floors content in my memories just for a while

My feet feel the cool of the hardwood as I move towards the outer doorway
Now on the porch I spy my old chair; in this light it looks silver gray
Pulling my robe around me I curl on its comforting wicker
Lean forward and light a candle, then sit back and watch it flicker

I feel as if something might happen as I sit quietly in the glow
The big picture window looks out on the lawn to my garden that blooms below
The night creatures venture outside feeling safe in their ebony blind
I sense that the quiet velvet night has a message that I will find

Finally, I see what awaits me walking the grounds, so near
His rich creamy coat and pale amber eyes show nary a trace of fear
The great wolf pauses and regards me, then fades into fragrant spruce trees
And I know that his sighting is something rare and just what my wild heart needs

He is free and untamed as I like to be when I feel the call to create
He's not tied to the ways of others and fully embraces his fate
He came this way to remind me that I need to be steady and true
To the things that bring me life's joy in all that I say and do

Some nights I walk the floors like this when I cannot stay in my dreams
I take in the creatures and feelings of night as they glow in the silent moonbeams
It's a magical time when my inner voice speaks to desires of my deepest heart
And a chance to create for the sensitive me, to nourish and guide my art

How many times in our lives have we ached to stay in bed on a cold winter day, nestled in a warm cocoon of covers, not ever wanting to emerge? But we do, because we need to get the job done. The yen to snuggle up follows us all day until we can return to the comfort of our cozy beds. Some days are just like that!

I Don't Want to Get Up

My body feels old and I have a bed head
And I want to stay snuggled deep in my bed
But the cows are a-calling
'Cause their feed needs some hauling
So I have to get up instead
The chilled floor just fills me with dread

... Barbie-Jo Smith

My pants are laying where I threw them on the floor
And my shirt is in a pile over there by the door
I wish I had a servant who would do my chores for me
But I'm here all alone with no one else you see
So I throw back the covers and prepare to meet the day
But I really, really don't want to get up from the hay

I stumble to the kitchen to make a cup of Joe
While I fumble with my boots that I'll wear out in the snow
My jacket slips on neatly while I sip my warm coffee
And pull on my mittens that my mother made for me
And step out on the porch to greet the crisp new day
I should just play hooky, then in my sheets I'd lay

But the cattle are waiting for me to see them through
And are greeting me with their long low moos
So out to the barn I shuffle my long spindly legs
And grab my well-worn chaps from the wooden peg
To saddle and bridle and blanket and spurs
Of course, my warm blankets are what I'd prefer

I swing into my saddle as my horse stands for me
Then, it's out to the range—I've got cattle to feed
And when the job is done I will come back to the farm
And put my horse in with hay that will keep her good and warm
Then when the day's done and I'm duly fed
I'll jump right back into my warm cozy bed

When you must live your life by the whims of Mother Nature, you must also be ready to adopt Plan B. Time management and a good long list are the hallmarks of someone whose life is ruled by the weather. However, don't forget the soothing balm of several cups of good strong cowboy coffee!

A Rainy Farm Day

I lay awake in my bed, hearing the rain
I guess my plans for the day will change
Patters fall gently against my window pane
Guess I'll be working on another type of range

That's the way it is when you live on the land
The weather dictates how things turn out, you see
Mother Nature just laughs at well laid plans
So you learn to just go with Plan B

Today I was going to the field to mow hay
Lay it down to dry sweet and fresh
I guess that will wait for another day
So it's back to my unending chore list

There are always many chores to get done
When you live on a big old farm
The big trick is to be flexible with time
So things don't fall so far behind

So I pull on my jeans and head down to the kitchen
Fresh coffee in hand I reach for my list
There's a gate in the barn that could use some fixing
But also some work to do on the grist

If I grind the grist now then I can bake some fresh bread
And when the rain's done I can do outside work
Later a fresh treat with some good apple spread
With fresh coffee I'll put onto perk

So I head out to the range; the one here in the kitchen
Fresh bread is a coming for me and my sweet
I pull down my bowls and commence to mixing
A rainy day Plan B; most surprising treat

I just love autumn!

Autumn Afternoon

Enjoying the sun I lay back in my chair
While the late autumn breeze ruffles wisps of my hair
Wasps play their symphony buzzing away
And butterflies land on the flowers as they sway

I'm surrounded by nature and happy to be
Sitting here in the shade of the crab apple tree
I'll keep this sweet memory when winter winds churn
Till once more the glory of autumn returns

We're very lucky to have a trailer where we can enjoy being out in nature but retreat at the end of the day to the creature comforts of home.

Camping in the Trailer

We awaken in dry warmth, snuggling in our bed
Waiting for the coffee pot to perk
Memories of the old times drift back into our heads
Of soaking rain and blowing winds and work

These days we have our trailer and we're as cozy as can be
With all the latest gadgets that give more time for play
Now our chairs sit in the shade of a big old elm tree
A far cry from all the gear back in "the day"

Back then we had a canvas tent with leaky zipper doors
So we prayed for many dry and sunny days
As it rained the water rose deeper on the floors
And we feared our beds would simply float away

Now we have a queen sized bed and lights for us to see
When nature calls us from covers snug and warm
No longer do we trip and fall when we have to "p".....
Or stub a toe and cry out in alarm

Breakfast is a wonder with a table all set up
No need to chip damp kindling and choke on all the smoke
Just flick a switch, cook the food, sipping java in a cup
That seems a whole lot better for us older camping folk

In the old days I fried up breakfast on the open fire
The wood smoke made the food taste just so great
The simple things of life was my only real desire
Like piles of bacon set upon my plate

In my old plaid housecoat, Lordy what a sight
Slicking up the dishes and hanging out the clothes
I was happy just puttering from morn till evening light
Then to sit and let the fire warm my toes

Do we miss those days we ask ourselves sometimes
Yes, but we were young and strong and zippy years ago
So now we love our trailer with amenities so fine
'Cause we're senior campers now don't you know

For anyone who has experienced the heartbreak of losing an identical twin—
it's a loss like no other.

Madeleine's Twin

Madeleine's twin has been gone now, two years
A long time, yet, just yesterday
Her absence is marked by her dear sister's tears
Who grieves for her, wishing to say...

I love you, dear Helen, but you've gone off so far
Of me you're forever a part
I miss you, my dear one, your loss made a scar
That presses down over my heart

Where are you now? Are you ok?
I want you here right by my side
Just for a time so that I can say
That our souls remain tightly tied

I miss having you at the end of the line
When I phone you on each new day
I'm anxious to know that you're doing fine
Now that you're so far away

I feel such sadness that you're not right there
Beside me as always you were
Now my days are filled with pain hard to bear
And life seems an awful blur

... Barbie-Jo Smith

We had so much to live for my girl, you and I
Now I struggle to get through the day
I am lost in my sorrow and it's hard to get by
I feel like I've just lost my way

But somewhere inside me, I know this to be
That your time here had come to a close
You were called to do things that I cannot see
So heavenward your splendid soul rose

You were summoned beyond by a special command
To be closer each day to our Lord
To be touched by his love and again by his hand
And this was your finest reward

I miss you, my twin, from the depths of my soul
And I know that one day I'll see you again
But for now I must stay to learn, that I know
Right here on this earthly plane

I know you love me with all of your heart
And you watch over me through the long night
So I'm happy to live life, doing my part
Till I rise towards the loving white light

Helen, dear one, you're the lucky twin
To do heavenly work with our Lord
I miss you. I love you. I'll see you again.
I give you my solemn word.

Sometimes it takes a monumental occasion for us to understand that we're never alone.

Angel Rider

Snow swirled around us and we were just so cold and tired
My horse stumbled yet again on this dark unending ride
Then I felt him next to me, a glowing loving presence
Something I could not describe; this ethereal loving essence

The day had been tough, harder than it should have been
Calves born in early spring had scattered to the wind
Bolted from their mothers in a wild and desperate flight
I searched for them throughout the day and into this bleakest night

Where had they gone; they're too young and alone
Their mothers lowed for them to come back to what was their home
Safe and warm with their moms, with warm milk to gently soothe
Like the way I feel when in my flannel shirt, soft and worn smooth

A lone cougar had spooked them to run so far
With the hope of having several meals close by her cubs and lair
And now they're lost somewhere out there in the rocky hills
Directly in harm's way, lost and scared; likely to be killed

My job was to find them, so on my trusty horse I went
But the weather changed so fast that my horse was quickly spent
Just in trying to walk through the building drifts of snow
And now we're lost far from familiar land that I remember and know

So here we are in the swirl and losing heat and heart
Then I felt Him beside me and it gave me quite a start
My horse sensed his presence, too, and broke into a canter
Whatever was happening, my heart felt better

It seemed as though an unseen guide had fully taken over
Leading my horse towards the cliffs like some giant unseen drover
"Have faith," he whispered. "You'll ride this storm out
In safety and comfort with your horse; let me be your scout."

So he led us to a cave that I didn't know before
The walls were tall, it was warm and dry with grass spread the floor
A bright warm fire burned in a rocky ring of stones
And I sensed that we were very safe in our temporary home

I dismounted and shook snow from my sodden denim jeans
My horse lowered his head and nibbled the grass around his feet
Then as if right on cue, our guide stepped from the rocky shadows
I stared at his aura that radiated in the stony hollow

He said, "Don't be afraid; I know of your plight
And I'm here to help you on this frozen night."
He smiled then and stepped aside, revealed a bigger space
And as I peered deep into the depths I heard a tiny voice

As my eyes got used to the murky depths I began to realize
That I was looking at the lost calves, right before my eyes
I turned to him asking what had happened this night
He smiled at me and began to slowly fade away from my sight

I lost all sense of fear as I remembered his peaceful face
And I knew my life was spared when he led us to this place
But more than simply leading us to warmth, this much I know
I sensed deep inside my heart that he had also saved my soul

Next day the sun shone so bright it pained my weary eyes
The calves walked behind my horse making little cries
Until they saw their mamas and their woolly loving care
My job was done; we're almost home; I want my easy chair

The years have rolled by since that night of cruel weather
When our lives were saved by the heavenly stranger
I've thought long and hard about that long ago night
When I stood under the beam of that holy light

How much different I am as in faith I have grown
And am grateful for the seeds that the stranger has sown
When I ride the range now two go along you see
I have faith that the stranger is always near to me
For I feel him as he rides by my side
A silent, loving and heavenly guide

... Barbie-Jo Smith

Composting is nothing new in the world. People have been doing it for millennia. Whether you dig it directly into your garden, put it in a fancy container or dump it in a pile in an out of the way spot, it all does the same wonderful thing. Where garden waste once was, in time, rich loam emerges—a gift from the Mother Nature.

Compost

On the counter sits a pail that's quite nondescript
It's so very plain that you might not even see
But underneath the lid if you give it a flip
Is a concoction of trendy ecco tea

Banana peels, coffee grounds, and orange rinds
Egg shells and tea bags, too
Sitting together for a prescribed time
They cook up a powerful brew

Whenever the pail is bursting its seams
I take a walk in the woods with a secret smile
To a mound in the grass where activity teems
There I add the new contents to the growing pile

A pitch fork is leaning against a big old tree
So I grab it and dig all around the dump site
Mixing the refuse; it's ever changing, you see
Into soil rich with earthy delights

I do this all summer till late into fall
When the soil dries out and hardens
I dig under the pile for a rich earthy haul
To spread on my lawns and garden

This rich garden mix worth more than your gold
Giving back to the world in a way that means most
The return to the earth is a hundred fold
The value of rick dark compost

Calving time is very busy. Sometimes problems arise, which need the intervention of the rancher or even the veterinarian. However, most cows birth their calves the way nature has arranged. Once the process is underway, it goes very quickly, so if you want to observe, don't turn your head!

Down in the Pasture

The sun has just risen and I'd better get moving
Crawl from my bed snug where I lay
Out in the pasture there's a whole of mooing
What could be happening to start off my day

I pull on my boots and grab my plaid shirt
And saunter on down to the pasture
A heifer stands wild eyed but doesn't seem hurt
What's happening, dear girl, I ask her

Two tiny legs with miniature feet
Protrude from her bovine back quarters
She strains to deliver her baby so sweet
And it's arriving in very short order

I watch in amazement as I always do
Each time I see this occur
The wonder of life being renewed
Brings tears to my eyes every time for sure

That sweet heifer heaves and gives one last gasp
And like magic her baby arrives
Slides from her body to the soft pasture grass
A tiny wet creature with huge liquid eyes

Mama sniffs at her baby and licks his wee nose
Then she gives a soft moo from deep within her chest
Her tongue begins licking her baby's damp coat
While he gazes in wonder at this strange new place

The licking encourages the baby to rise
On spindly new legs that wobble like frail reeds
But this baby bull is destined to thrive
To grow strong and sire more of his breed

He's now looking for food when up on his feet
His mother provides her baby's first meal
He found rich warm milk as he pulled on her teat
And they both softly lowed in bovine zeal

And so it all goes time and again
The miracle of birth in the bovine world
Then I glance to the left across the home pen
And here comes another—a tiny wee girl

REPRINTS

I chose to add this section because even though the next 7 poems have appeared in my other books, I felt they also belonged in a collection that reflects my country heart. I hope you will indulge me as I present them again.

This poem was inspired from a true experience that I had. For those of you who have ever tried to load an ornery bull, you will recognize the struggle.

Loading the Bull

He was pretty cagey and learned how to veer
So he missed the procedure that makes a bull into steer
Living in the field with the heifers was a whirl
That's how nobody noticed that he wasn't a girl

Time ticked on by and they grew eating hay
The heifers would all be mothers one day
Our boy grew the biggest 'cause his gender made him so
Pretty soon his size would let someone know

The Vet checked the heifers but this one seemed quite strange
But then there are all sorts of cows on the open range
While all the cows 'cept one was growing a wee calf
A closer look made the Vet howl a big huge laugh

... Barbie-Jo Smith

It was that second look that revealed the mistake
This is a young bull—his laughter made him shake
There will never be a calf inside this huge barge
But you'd better watch him closely, he's awfully doggone large

Now some bulls are gentle and handle very well
But this young bull had attitude from living with the gals
A danger he'd become to all those far and wide
It was time to take him for that long, long ride

He would go on the trailer and down the great long road
To the stockyard to wait with others till there was a full load
To take them to market and make no mistake
He would make juicy burgers and nice big lean steaks

Tags in ears was the rule to the line
And this proved a bit of an issue
For winter had been harsh on this young, strong bovine
It had frozen away most of the tissue

So Dwayne and Tom then devised a great chase
To herd the young bull without fear
In the press he would stand with great grace
While they tagged what was left of an ear

The bull, of course, had other plans
About how he would spend his day
He was not ready to be put in the stand
Preferring to munch on sweet hay

The boys had been down at the barn for an hour
Convincing the bull to behave
We gals were wondering if things had gone sour
Knowing that all three were brave

But enough was enough and worry crept in
So I wandered on down to the barn
There was crashing & snorting and all sorts of din
Which aroused some serious concern

I crept closer to the corral gate
And out charged Tom with a grin on his face
And perched up high to watch and wait
All was not over in this bovine race

Now the struggle was down to sheer pride
As Tom set the trailer gate, boy, was he bold
A whoop and a shout from Duane inside
Sent the bull up the ramp and into the hold

He charged on board with a tag in his ear
And the boys sat back with a grin
The work had been hard and deserved a good cheer
But that ornery bull was in

Ye haw, the job was over at last
And I couldn't believe their luck
From the noise and the clamour I was certain
That the bull would be driving the truck

So soon after that we craved something delicious
What was our range chef to make?
Something that had once been noisy and vicious
But now it was just meat on a plate
Yum Yum!

... Barbie-Jo Smith

Everyone should have the chance to be snowbound with someone they love.

Spring Storm

Soft light filters through the blind on the window in our room
I stir a bit, stretch and find a change in our warm cocoon
It's morning and yet far too early to rise and face the day
What made me rouse I wonder, then I hear my husband say

Darlin' it's springtime in Alberta and you can never know
What will greet you in the morn, bright sun or heavy snow
Mother Nature holds the cards and makes her final choice
We're just along for the ride and do not have a voice

She'll pick a sunny day for all of us to have
Or she'll throw a late snow storm at us and really have a laugh
But anyway she chooses she helps to make us strong
It's her world we're living in and we just ride along

So he said as he stretched and yawned and chuckled very lightly
It's up to us to make the most of what she brings us nightly
He laughed out loud and threw the blanket high above our heads
Then pulled me down beside him, cuddled warmly in our bed

Yes, Spring time can be tricky, now don't you go and scoff
Everything we planned today will have to be put off
Last night brought a foot of snow and trapped us for the day
But, we don't care, we're warm and snug and here we're going to lay!

Ancient Man and Life Blood are companion pieces that have travelled many miles with me and also appeared in my first book. Life Blood remains on permanent museum display. I had the great honour of reading Ancient Man to distinguished Elders at an Aboriginal Council. While I am proud to have written these pieces, they are really the heartthrob of the people working through my hands.

Ancient Man

You've come to tell me something, Ancient man of the land
Teach me what you know, please help me understand
What your people felt and how they lived their lives
Tell me, ancient man, about the old ways to survive

Your life and times are real to me, Ancient man of the land
Your message is important as our time is close at hand
"Mother Earth is sacred, do not harm her land"
I did not know this, wise one. I'm so sorry, Ancient man

I took her gifts for granted, I did not know the way
Now you're here to tell me just how I can repay
My debt to Mother Earth and Grandmother Moon, as well
Speak to my heart, old one, all you have to tell

Ancient Man Speaks

"Hunting, fishing, living, dying; those things that we do well
The people have been living here too many years to tell
But now the strange new ones claim our ancient land
It's hard to watch my people fade by another's hand"

"It was sad to see the old ways die," said the Ancient Man
"I saw my people, with my heart, grieving for their land
But from the ashes of our loss, new living must progress
Bringing with it understanding, healing and success"

... Barbie-Jo Smith

"You have your place in history," the Ancient Man replied
"You opened up this country, standing side by side
But what you missed for all to see is this was once our home
We were always here forever free to roam"

"There is a way to live here, white and red together
Standing strong to serve our hearts for now and so forever
Respect the Earth and all she gives to those that you hold dear
Never take without giving and you will have no fears"

"See the world for all it is on this glorious day
Always feel the throbbing life that shows you the true way
Never take for granted these gifts that have been given
Always hold your life in awe, it's here for us, the living"

"Together our nations must work hard, standing side by side
To solve our many problems and lovingly abide
In harmony with each other and Mother Earth, as well
No more tears and sorrow, to them we say farewell"

The Ancient Man had spoken, his words rang loud and clear
Work together to preserve the ways that all of us hold dear
Respect each other and our own to make our nations strong
Forever in this wondrous place where we all belong

Life Blood

Thundering herds have crossed our land since ancient times ago
We tracked them through both loam and sand
Our life blood buffalo

Bellowing bulls guard giant herds; lowing cows call soft eyed calves
Perfect harmony seems the word
Our life blood buffalo

Tall and strong, exciting, alive; enormous heads toss to and fro
They give their all that we survive
Our life blood buffalo

Live through seasons harsh and rough; push through ice and snow
Majestic, tall, strong and tough
Our life blood buffalo

Run forever strong and free; to them Creator did bestow
The best of creatures land and sea
Our life blood buffalo

They leave their tracks deep in hearts; they are our brothers of the soul
Bringing life for us to start
Our life blood buffalo

When white man came upon the scene with guns and knives to show
They nearly stripped the land all clean
Of our life blood buffalo

But from the ashes of despair the sacred calf we know
Rising son taught us to care
For our life blood buffalo

This white calf is the future hope as winds of change do blow
To teach white and red to learn to cope
Our life blood buffalo

Because of him I hear and see what life gives me to know
My brother to the heart of me
My lifeblood—buffalo

... Barbie-Jo Smith

I love this poem and have added it into all of my books. It was fun to write, but also honours the connection I have to the land when I grow my garden and then preserve its bounty.

Pickles

Oh yum, yum how I love to eat
Home canned pickles so tart and so sweet
Onions and sugar and spices galore
Make taste buds zingy and shouting for more

Deep in the garden hidden by leaves
Cucumbers reside awaiting to be
All kinds of treats packed tightly in jars
Seasoned just right, small, green super stars

Dill pickles, small and flavoured with salt
Garlic and peppers and vinegar malt
Set on the shelves till they're ready to eat
I can't wait to devour these savoury treats

Mustard ones laced with spices and sweets
Often I use big rosy beets
To make bright red morsels to tickle the palate
I'd vote for these winners if I had a ballot

Cucumbers, corn, and broccoli, too
Cauliflower, onions, and dill that I strew
In sealers shiny and ready to cradle
All nature's treasures that I lovingly ladle

Tighten the tops and set them to cool
Survey the bounty from my canning stool
Odours that tease the nostrils and eyes
Winter will yield my work day's surprise

At the end of the day when my eyes cry big tears
From peeling the onions without my eye gear
And when fingers are wrinkled from washing new veggies
And my old work stool gave me a huge wedgie
All sinuses cleared from inhaling the fumes
Of vinegar designed to clear any room
I survey the product of my long day of labour
My love of the garden and veggies I savour
I know I will do this again every year
Till I'm too old to see, smell, and yes, even hear

Some folks look forward to a winter vacation
When weather is harsh in this our great nation
But I think of summer and all that is sweet
And nature's great pickles chomped' tween my front teeth!

... Barbie-Jo Smith

On a hot summer afternoon, after a cattle roundup, I started thinking about how it was for those who worked the land long before our time. It's not hard to think of the terrible beauty of this land where people must be prepared for any event in order to do what they must to survive. My cowboy was a special man for he knew how lucky he had been to have experienced everything about the life he loved so much.

His message is really the timeless lessons about life.

A Cowboy's Story

I was but a youngster then
When I rode my first long drive
A saddle tramp years two and ten
How did I stay alive?
My horse that knew much more than me
My buddies on the trail
My natural talent they did see
Saved me without fail
I look back with weathered eyes
My memories still enduring
Those times, at first, a huge surprise
But the life was so alluring
The heat, the cold, the rain and snow
They often broke my heart
But this life was all I came to know
Open range where I got my start

Long hot days with dust and sweat
As I drive the cattle further west
Into the prairie to seek new grass
To feed them and to help them last
Through tough summer days with rain so slight
They're restless and quickly take to flight
Towards the river with its muddy mire
To quench their burning thirst desire

Sun scorched prairie yields little feed
To fulfil their overwhelming need
To grow strong and yet survive
This hostile climate and to thrive
Growing to be huge strong beasts
That will provide man's table feast
I drive them towards that finishing goal
Cash on the hoof, I very well know

How do cowboys, present and past
Toil and slave, yet seem to last
Through summer heat and drought and dust
Driving cattle as they must
The weather changing in a flash
Cruel storms and lightening hot as ash
Torrential rain that soaks the skin
And dampens the very soul within
Yet they carry on through night and day
For them there is no other way

My world seems filled with pestilence
Which demands my utmost vigilance
My savvy horse oft' snorts a warning
That wolves slink by in early morning
Snakes that strike with lightning speed
Taking down cow, man and steed
Sucking mud at river's edge
Claims those who step off the gravel ledge
And hoppers that chomp the last green grass
Competing with cattle to see who lasts
The competition for sustenance
Proves a delicate survival dance
Alkali water waiting to ruin
Careless cows that drink too soon
Stampedes that make the very earth rumble
And roar and shake and even tumble

But...

Who can have a life like this?
Hard work and yet so free
For this cowboy it means true bliss
Nature, but the space to be

Sunrise in the early morn
Coffee starts my day
For this life I was surely born
And hardships seem like play

Sure there are the searing things
When I question what I do
Some tragedies that the trail brings
But hardship is the glue
That makes good times outweigh the bad
And learning my whole existence
Brings value to the things I've had
That's why I go the distance

Sometimes I wonder why I'm here
And what I hope to learn
But then I glimpse a bounding deer
And I understand my yearn
For the freedom of this rugged land
And the creatures that in it dwell
My life is good and right at hand
My pride begins to swell

The cattle's ever moving tide
An eagle on the wing
My steady steed on which I ride
The peace this life can bring
No matter what you do in life
Choose what grows your heart
Be it easy or filled with strife
From your true course never part
You'll become one strong and wise
At lessons life will show
But you'll receive the biggest prize
A cowboy's heart and soul

Oh the things that I have seen
Bad things, good, and in between
But on our great enduring land
This boy became a man... A Cowboy

... Barbie-Jo Smith

Three Friends was inspired by a picture given to me by my brother-in-law, Frank Hale. He knew I would love it and he was right. It features a cowboy out in a storm with his horse and dog, searching for a lost calf. When I saw the picture I felt as though I could step into it and join the friends on that stormy night, when Joe sounded the alarm and Dan carried the cowboy through the storm. No matter how difficult the task, they stuck together to get the job done. After their work years were over they remained together. I hope you enjoy their story and their eternal friendship.

Three Friends

I looked to the sky and saw foreboding grey
As flakes of new snow started falling my way
The herd had gone out somewhere in the hills
To find themselves shelter from the bone numbing chills

But this was the time when the babies were born
Tiny wee creatures, brand new but still strong
Like their ancestors, bred to this land
But still not a match for the storm that's at hand

I knew I must find them way out on the prairie
So I made my arrangements to ride and to hurry
To find little beasts and their parents, too
And save this year's herd; oh, the wind how it blew

I walked to the barn and saw my cayuse
We were a strong team when the cattle broke loose
My horse stood ready to do all that I asked
Always my partner, up for each task

Dan's ears twitched forward as I quickly drew near
Soft brown eyes followed as I gathered our gear
He rumbled a whinny deep from his chest
Anxious to leave and to give me his best

My dog arose swiftly from his warm bed of hay
Eager to join us to search on that day
For calves, unprotected from cruel winds and snow
We three formed a team, sharing all that we know

Tossing the blanket and saddle aloft
Tightened the cinch and bridle up top
I swung myself up and was ready to go
Out to the storm, me, Dan, and Joe

Cantering quickly across frozen range
We reached the white hills so cold and so strange
Heads down against driving wind and cruel snow
And inched through the valley way down deep below
We soon found the herd crushed against a rock wall
Driven that way by the blinding snowfall
I nudged Dan forward through the punishing weather
Hoping to find them there all together

The cows turned to look when we rode up beside
They were cold and exhausted with ice on their hides
One mother stood lonely without her wee baby
Could I find him for her—I wonder, just maybe

Dan wheeled around as if reading my mind
Joe sniffed the air to see what he could find
I peered forward through the cold driving snow
Hoping to sense where a small creature could go

Is that a noise I heard through the scream
Of winds blowing strongly—perhaps, it's a dream
But Dan perked his ears up and Joe barked alarm
Was there a calf here so far from the barn

I cocked my head up while the wind raged and blew
And through the loud noise I heard a small moo
Off to the left the sound came again
The call of a calf, it was weak, but still plain

Joe gave a bark and Dan pawed the ground
We galloped through snow and then we soon found
The tiny wee calf legs all tangled in sage
Holding him tightly just like a cage

His coat was all sodden and he gave a small cry
His soft eyes said help me, I don't want to die
I leapt off my horse and pulled at the brush
His legs came untangled, all in a rush

Joe sniffed the calf and wagged his great tail
Dan stamped his hoof on the frozen, packed trail
I knelt on the ground and felt his leg bones
Our calf was all right, just tired and alone

Joe nudged the calf with his wet friendly nose
To urge him to rise before his legs froze
The calf mooed at Joe with his little calf voice
But stand he must try; he had no other choice

Dan nickered softly and bent his great head
To nuzzle the calf and to urge him to stand
That must have been what that tiny one needed
For he struggled and stood alone quite unimpeded

He was up on his feet and I knew he'd survive
If the herd moved together on this cold cattle drive
We could drive them all home through the snow and the ice
Warmth, food and shelter would surely entice

I lifted the calf up in my strong arms
High in the saddle above any harm
Dan understood it was time to get going
Return to the ranch away from the snowing

Tail wagging high, excited and keen
Joe ran ahead through the steep dark ravine
Driving them home towards warmth and good food
Something the hungry herd would not elude

Close to the ranch the cows smelled the hay
And fresh straw for bedding on which they could lay
They trotted right into the barn and began
To eat to their pleasure for me, Joe, and Dan

We had walked home that day through the cold nasty weather
Teamwork and luck kept us all safe together
Joe, Dan, and me and the herd plus one baby
We knew we were lucky to make it home safely

Over the years we went out in more storms
Always to find the herd and bring it home
My trusty old friends right by my side
To be with me always, to comfort and guide

We always did well at what we did best
We were a team and we were so blessed
To live on the range and have freedom at hand
And wander across this beautiful land

... Barbie-Jo Smith

How did we manage that night long ago
What was the magic we shared—I don't know
I have thought of that time now over the years
The warmth of my feelings oft brought me to tears

My beautiful Dan with his coat of deep red
White centre stripe adorned his huge head
Plush mane and tale set him apart
And soft dark brown eyes revealed his great heart

My trusty old Joe with long flowing coat
Pale golden white, like the colour of oats
His tail full and bushy, which he held high
To signal his pleasure or wag a good-bye

I rode good old Dan for years on the range
With Joe at our side till there seemed a change
In all three of our lives as we lessened in strength
And knew that our work years had a certain time length

So the three of us settled for the rest that we earned
For the roundup we sometimes earnestly yearned
But we're still here together Joe, Dan, and me
Dear friends together, happy and free

Joe lays by my feet in the morning sunshine
Dan grazes nearby, happy and fine
I sit with feet up a-whittling away
Just three old friends passing each day

End of Reprints

We all have roots, whether they be the tapestry of families, the rich relationship of friends, the support of community, our spirituality or connection to the land. We don't stand alone. We are a composite of those who have gone before.

Roots

As I walked back to the pasture on a hot summer day, my eyes fell on the big old oak tree that stood like a solitary beacon, surrounded by wheat. How many times had I walked this way without taking the time to stop and really look at this giant? Now, I marvelled at how many generations it had stood tall and proud like a lookout over the land. As I neared, I looked down on the roots that undoubtedly ran deep, but were also visible as they broke through the turf like massive arms. The fields were now tilled well away from the old one to ensure that its roots weren't damaged by machinery. This old friend was respected, revered and preserved. I mused that this giant was like family—new generations branching out above while past generations ran deeply into the ground to provide a strong anchor.

Just as this magnificent tree had begun from an acorn that may have randomly rooted in that place, so had my grandfathers, six times over, taken root. Each in turn, standing together with his wife, toiled and worked the land while raising large families. Alongside them grew the oak tree, sending out roots below and branches above in the same way the farmer and his wife puts their roots down, raised their children, begetting the following generations.

Stepping closer I looked into the canopy and saw scars on the bark, crossed branches rubbing against each other and branches broken short; reminders that the oak had weathered many storms. In the same way, families have scars as they experienced great sickness, drought, storms and lost and missing members. Their roots become larger as they dig in during adversity. Like the oak tree who has knots and knobs on its roots where it has been brushed by equipment, families also have scars and imperfections where wounds healed.

Sometimes the oak tree lost part of its canopy when the wind blew like a gale, driving snow, hail and rain its way. When the top broke, the roots responded to grow stronger and send out new shoots to grow into new branches. Similarly, families suffered the loss of loved ones through wars and sickness, but the roots of the family were still there, holding it firm.

In time, the family responded by filling in the gaps where their loved ones once were and creating more new branches in the form of marriages and children. There are lots of pits and scrapes as families struggle to find their way and suffer through life's calamities, but their roots keep them strong, anchoring them throughout life.

We all have roots. Some run very deep in one place. Others are shallow as families move around to re-establish or come from other parts of the world. We're all a composite of the ones who lived before us. Their traits shuffle and re-shuffle throughout the generations to produce new composites—new people—different, but linked by the roots of their families, friends, and places in time. The ones who went before aren't gone. They live in us and we go on. My forbearers are a part of me and I'm proud to be a part of them.

The Road of Life

The road of life has twists and turns and that's an actual fact
But we only learn this after we've walked for years along the track
By then we've reached an age when we begin to understand
What life is all about, this gift given by God's hand

When we're younger our lives move quickly, and fully occupied
We sense within ourselves that somewhere we have a loving guide
But our busy lives pull us to and fro—we don't stop to really see
So we hurry onwards through the years like an uncontrolled banshee

But as we age and life begins to take a slower pace
We're allowed to see the patterns that our lives have slowly traced
It's then we really start to live with feeling and with more love
For ourselves and our loved ones with help from the One above

Our thoughts travel back in time, through all those wondrous years
Filled with memories that bring us laughter and yes, as well, some tears
But we also have a deeper knowledge now of how the road unwinds
And it's in that learning that in the end, it's ourselves we finally find

And so the road of life goes on and we begin to see
What lies behind its gentle curves for you and also me
And in that glimpse the meaning of our journey comes quite clear
That the road we walked was meant to be, and our Guide was always near

Author Credits

<u>Dream Write Publishing Ltd., Sherwood Park, Alberta</u>
A Country Gal in the City 2011
Things Were Going Fine Till We Hit the Rapids November, 2015
Echoes of a Country Heart November, 2015

<u>Polar Expressions Publishing Ltd., Maple Ridge, British Columbia</u>
Canadian Anthologies of poetry and short stories

Solitude,2009
Ink Spots, 2011
Harvest, 2012
Before the Frost, 2013
The Warbler's Song, 2014
Wherever We Roam, 2015
The Journey, 2010
The Calling, 2011
Setting the Scene, 2012
The Sun Shall Rise, 2013
That Golden Summer, 2014
Waking Dawn, 2015

<u>The Poetry Institute of Canada, Victoria, British Columbia</u>
Canadian Anthologies of poetry and short stories
Island Magic, 2014
Mists of Morning, 2014
National Poetry Contest, 2014, 3rd Prize
National Creative Writing Contest, 2014, Award of Excellence
A Tracery of Trees, 2015
Spring's Gentle Rain, 2015

<u>Alberta 55+ Summer Games Writing Contest</u>
Provincial Gold Medal, Poetry, 2015
Zone Bronze Medal, Poetry, 2015

Libraries Archives
National Archives of Canada
Strathcona Public Library
Calgary Public Library
Saskatoon Public Library

Watch for Barbie-Jo's next books:

"Everything Let Loose at Once" and "Another Piece of Pie, Please!"

Released by Dream Write Publishing in 2016